QUICK TO BOLT

QUICK
TO BOLT

ᔰ POEMS ᔰ

Mary Fister

GREEN WRITERS PRESS | *Brattleboro, Vermont*

Printed in the United States

10 9 8 7 6 5 4 3 2 1

Green Writers Press is a Vermont-based publisher whose mission is to spread a message of hope and renewal through the words and images we publish. Throughout we will adhere to our commitment to preserving and protecting the natural resources of the earth. To that end, a percentage of our proceeds will be donated to environmental activist groups. Green Writers Press gratefully acknowledges support from individual donors, friends, and readers to help support the environment and our publishing initiative.

GReen
wriTers
press

Giving Voice to Writers & Artists Who Will Make the World a Better Place

Green Writers Press | Brattleboro, Vermont
www.greenwriterspress.com

ISBN: 979-8-9865324-2-4

PRINTED ON RECYCLED PAPER BY BOOKMOBILE.
BASED IN MINNEAPOLIS, MINNESOTA, BOOKMOBILE BEGAN AS A DESIGN AND
TYPESETTING PRODUCTION HOUSE IN 1982 AND STARTED OFFERING PRINT SERVICES IN 1996.
BOOKMOBILE IS RUN ON 100% WIND- AND SOLAR-POWERED CLEAN ENERGY.

CONTENTS

III.

ACKNOWLEDGMENTS

Acknowledgment is gratefully given to the following journals in which some of these poems in slightly different form appeared:

America, "For the Feast of the Epiphany"

Ascent, "The Physics of Pure Moment"

Berkeley Poetry Review, "With Round Voices Leading"

Cream City Review, "For a Few Trees"

Epiphany, "Avian Rapture," "Galahad Blue"

The Fourth River, "Stronger Than Winter"

The Jabberwock Review, "Insomnia"

Laurel Review, "Freshening"

The Little Magazine, "Whispering Campaign"

The Massachusetts Review, "Parting Shots"

Natural Bridge: A Journal of Contemporary Literature, "Blonde Oak," (published under the title, "Anniversary Table") and "Uncertain Perches"

The Naugatuck Review, "Opening the Drawer"

New Delta Review, "The Korl Sculptor"

Ploughshares, "Sounding"

The Seattle Review, "Dotted Swiss"

Southern Humanities Review, "Aunt Eleanor" (originally published under the title "Dreaming Her Sea-Worthy")

Sou'wester, "Farmer by the Sea,"

Tar River Poetry, "Morning Enough"

Volt, "So Does This Canticle for Wind"

I

NANTUCKET BLUFF

Someone must have set it so—
this lone Adirondack chair
on a whiskered bluff
where sea blots sky.

How many visits
to get the angle right?
There had to be
a giving over

as sand splintered
the chair until it
sunk no more and anyone
could lean,

then lean back,
sigh out last year's bitter rains.
Or was it tossed
like sea-wrack and spawn,

kelp bladders,
scallop-shuck and straw?
And what of the lone beachcomber
dallying here,

her sorrow bottlenecked
at the sandbar during low tide?
She walks through
brief tidal pools.

Eddies rush her.
Mollusks scribble under run-off.
Her tracks fill in
with Arcturus' glint.

As shells are buffed
to porcelain,
her losses drift, tilt.
She gives over, spills.

SOUNDING

Already the leaden sky dissolves
and changes into a red-orange
plume on water—

as if our low-gear motor
mixes magnificent pigments
that funnel in,

then diffuse. And even though
we home in on a pocket
of river-must

where the anchor
will take hold,
that leavening

distance so slow
in coming gives a sense
of leaving for good.

From sea, some trees
spread flat as crewcuts,
others stoop under

the wind's greatcoat,
another straight as a girder
(that singular ascension,)

all on one shore!
So it's as courters
we float this slow

tidal feed, crouch
close as we can
to the soundless glint

of fireflies, a buoy's
undertones, and the skittish
peal from an osprey's nest

where the rev slows
and we drop anchor . . .
We spread an embroidered tablecloth

of mismatched threads
over the engine house
for our dinner

of sandwiches, cherries,
and wine. An *entre-deux-mers*
raised in toast

to soften the ospreys;
this odd coincidence
between name and

teetery locale.
Water-locked, we know
anywhere is possible

if we follow
that keen retriever
slicing the water,

limp duck in his soft mouth,
as we were once
caught off-guard,

glinting as one dim signal
where we gathered
our spavined hearts.

CLOSED FOR RIPENING

That leggy midsummer day
                    had already walked on.
You joining me unexpected.
We roamed from bush to bush,
out of earshot,
                    in that tilted grove.
Strange how we drifted differently—
my eye drawn to the blue
hidden in shadowed pools
on the lowest branches
                    with mown hay still clinging.
Your eye was haphazard, uncertain,
as you tested the give
                    of each reluctant cluster.

Then you rushed at me, held
                    the hurt I'd been hoarding.
I let you hold it.
Then fruit, the flower's bruise,
tumbled to our buckets.
On those acres, blue was deeper,
fruit sweeter,
and when we tasted,
                    we were broken
open, joined to the bough,
supple with rupturing berries.

DOTTED SWISS

I longed to unravel
the whole bolt,
run through dunes
with a sheer, ice-blue kite
unwinding behind,
a windblown net
making a fresh catch
of a skywriter's alphabet.

I swore the only time
white turned so vapor-blue
and see-through-milky all at once
was on a postcard
my grandmother sent of mountain peaks,
her penned-in dot marking
how far she'd climbed,
and since I squinted hard for it,
I became invisible
just by searching.

One night after supper
its three uncut yards slid and skidded
on the dining room table
as my mother chalked
my skinny figure
along its folds.
She bent over me,
her mouth
stuffed with pushpins,
barked out garbled orders

to keep turning
so she could erase exactly
where my breasts would one day be.

As she hung the now-resurrected
parts of my body on me,
I drew myself in tight
against its biting nap,
the dots imploding over
my flat bust,
and still I kept spinning and spinning,
longing to whip
those limp pieces
of my Communion dress
into mist I could disappear in.

Now the mist is too fine
to hide the quiet shuttle of my heart
as my mother lifts
my wedding veil,
with its scalloped border
of dotted swiss.
A snow-blue kite
fans out behind,
I am nothing but breath.

BLOND OAK

Light spills on our manuscript
of quarter-sawn core.

Morning's hard light scatters a burlesque
of just-tapped ore.

Gold jackknifes into black.
We wonder how sap

stowed light deep in roots,
ignited a riot of gain.

Afternoon light scrubs
amber linseed oil in.

What shows is unshowy—
ardor held at bay.

Limbs had enough cambre
to arch under birds

who came to roost.
When we come to it,

let our day out under candle,
it is a basin of terra-cotta light.

We are hushed
as a boat's underside. Quiet turns

its five-pointed pedestal.
Quiet buffs the story

of our first anniversary gift,
dropped in the heart

of our new life,
grainy with growth rings.

WHISPERING CAMPAIGN

It always begins with my aunt
leaning on the shelf above the stove,
cooking nothing, cast by the heat, no pockets
to warm her hands. She waits there, frozen almost, until the room
fills with their voices. I have a snapshot
of her youth, her russet-red hair, hidden in the attic.

They will be starting soon. I want to climb to the attic
where words vanish. Always the same: one aunt
had high blood pressure, the other lunch with the bishop. Around
    the stove
they screen their talks with *you-knows*. I want a pocket
with a kitten sewn in, so the whole room
might purr. Then I could eavesdrop, hear about the snapshot

the priest gave for absolution: Jesus by the sea. That snapshot
could buy my way through those gates, the Cadillac of attics.
Up there is a costume for every minute, young aunts
without opaque support hose, stoves
that cook beautiful fricassee, mere pockets
of gossip, not room after room.

They crowd around. Their whispers hiss. I leave for an empty room
with bristly horsehair chairs and side tables. Here a snapshot
of my mother's mother. She died while giving birth to her.
    Now the attic
is a green house full of orchids. Each day my aunt
leaves an orchid by that picture. That night the stove
had pots of boiling rags. She died with three oval stones in her pocket—

one for each daughter. I wondered how long it took them to pocket
their grief. And my mother, born an orphan, was there room
for her? I see three sisters in a snapshot,
each with French braids, arms linked. My mother stayed late in
    the attic
when she was young, waiting for her mother until my aunt
came for her, rocked her to sleep by the stove.

When the fire in the stove
died, she slipped her into a warm pocket
of blankets where her dreaming breathing filled the room.
She dreamed she walked by her mother's snapshot,
and she was held closer. She left in the attic
a nest of white feathers for my aunt.

My aunt leans over the stove, cast by its warmth,
while nieces dole out the latest gossip from their pockets. Through
    the attic
grate, they are a blurred snapshot, filling a room, whispering . . .

QUILTER'S CALLOUS

I wonder whether light
holds you

as you appliqué
this circle of quilt:

doves nest in lilies,
in twined arches,

as you tilt your quilter's hoop
and smooth a dove's neck,

then stitch lilies wide as a trumpet's bell.
I want to hope it does—

that for a moment you are in thrall
to the light behind you,

that those nights up late sewing
were not just building

enough callous to take on
this, your trickiest pattern:

the "Country Bride" where
doves round off in flight.

Mother, admit it hurts sometimes,
that stitching up loss with adages

does not patch up your hopes
for grandchildren, the trestle

your hoop is set on
can become deal and rickety

if too much pressure is brought to bear,
even light fails

if the moment is inopportune.
Still I will move under this quilt

with my husband, when you bear it
across my landing one day.

As it unfolds like sheet after sheet
of inscribed vellum, I will

prize the texture and comfort
of each rise and depression

set by your steady hand,
hole up in its balm

as I dream miles away
from your stitched vigil.

OPENING THE DRAWER

His hammers and wrenches,
jackknives, skinning knives,

screws, nails, and wing nuts
magnetized in a snarl.

Tincture of linseed oil,
freshly planed shavings,

salt smeared on a raccoon's brittle hide
could not blunt the gutting

which I know now
is the reek of giving birth.

And shoved deep, tangled in fishing line, catgut,
reels, bobbers, and lures,

were books titled *Beautiful Joe*
Old Yeller as though only boys

could know the mystery
of dogs and quests.

Our father built us identical desks that year.
I stuffed my drawers with letters,

poems to a boy who sat catty-corner,
diaries with sprung locks,

my clipped, ribboned braids,
autograph books that begged me to stay.

And sunlit photos of thoroughbreds,
restless along fence lines,

dog-eared volumes of *Misty*
and *The Black Stallion,* a frayed

halter of a horse
I'd never own.

I tagged along,
watched a friend ride,

her braids swayed
as she cleared another jump,

The drama was like
the trespass into my brother's

relics. I drew closer.
They were always out of reach.

TIGER LILIES

Next door at dusk
three retired professors hover above
tiger lilies sprawling
along the damp brick wall.
They argue about quotients,
stomp the lilies' roots,
ask what infinity
is divisible by.

Their trousers are rubbed
to a satin patina
from the tread and retracing
of theories in lecture halls.
If only they would come closer
thrall under the must
peat, clay and erasures,
smear their mouths
with a hue brief as fire.

The woman across the way
does not want to touch infinity,
rather, wants to pitch
their frayed rhetoric over,
dunk them slowly,
for she thinks of rows
and banks of tiger lilies
lining the way home.

She thinks all we remember
are paths and light,

the way of our going,
not where we finish
trembly and wind-chilled.
She imagines the old men
leaning in a little farther.
She swears just once
heat lightning volleys
among the blossoms.

WITH ROUND VOICES LEADING

Near shore the sun set
while the moon gained on.
They were the same roundness.
They were fixed at the same level,
ascending, descending.

Some say luster flung from prayers
pierces a bird's beak.
That one bird veers heavenward
with luminous banners. His preening
keeps the moon from tilting.

Others say a glassblower's breath
suspends the sun and moon,
that he blends our pent-up hopes
into molten globes.

Whatever craftsman fashioned this,
you travel a thin road
that leads to this sighting.
Its edge blurs
as you beachcomb grassy sea-manes.

There is the glow of the fishermen's light,
his pipe's shifting beacon.
As he mines fathoms for a tug
on his lure, you mine
fog for a sound undiluted.

Sea crabs slur water in.
Jellyfish, like dull, beached suns
pan colonies of periwinkles.
They nod in backwash.
Waves rake through,
dump shards, pocked wood.

Higher up in dunes
is a sea-urchin worn smooth
to a sequined pin cushion.
Still perfectly divided, it glistens.
In its dome is hushed
the roundness of vowels—
impossible not to salvage this weight,
the grace you hear in its name.

THE PHYSICS OF PURE MOMENT

The last strand of afternoon:
Pines are tusk-shadows on snow.
The click of splinters, branches.
Birds are stunned. I think

of volcano sides, how seeds grow
in lava beams. Possibly
at another stage become grist
for the glinting plow. Nothing tills

as evenly as oxen, steady
on ruddy turf. It's what keeps them.
So, too, eventually, pollen
knots in a kind of liaison:

always the sprig of half-eaten grass,
questions in those doleful eyes,
the curiosity in my standing
there. I think of where

this happens, of where birds move.
Like a slingstone, I go south
by degrees, informed by blind spots
as I look into the sun. I think

of carnivals, frenzied vendors,
that old Mayan asleep
behind his booth
of sweetened, colored, water.

He is dreaming in rows. Behind each row
is another pack that needs shifting
before it can make the pass.
He gives parcel of cloud

for ballast. He has dreamed
of leaving for years.
I want to wake him.
Tell him everything I've ever done

is trying to land. There is
a curtain of rain pulling
the sea up. That it is impossible
to know what falls.

ᔇ II ᔆ

AUNT ELEANOR

❧

You willed me books and a shelf.
Each binding is stretched
by remnants you stuck between pages—
pressed leaves, still-gaping snapdragons
in every shade, a letter describing
only mimosa, clippings on campaigns,
harvests, or Frost. On the shelf
is an oval stone— a blend
of ruddy red, grey and black.
You had it polished by a jeweler
when we found it, that day
you got me to believe
cats could sing in trees.

❧

Last night, the river flooded.
It left a ship stranded
like a sleeper that can't
turn over. Through fog,
the groans of rope
toiling in winches.

∾

Arborescent light, when sun
blares through leaves.
I kept your palm-sized books, let my legs
gum up with sap as I shinnied,
saved birch-bark for letter paper. You said
there are reasons for trees
craning toward the sun, for branches
accepting the burden of birds.
We heard roots drinking, a nick
in the overriding hum.

∾

A ship is being restored
outside my window.
There is distance in it.
Its keel cracks
without lapping water.
Its ribs bow
like a warped harp.

∾

We crossed a gorge on a swinging bridge,
barely pinned to boulders,
made of see-through slats.
You always put me in the lead
so I'd look more keenly on the other side
at the fine differences in leaf shapes,
colonies of ants drilling
under stones. Because of you,
the earth that covers you now reminds
its underside needs sunning.
Looking to the hills— I don't know
why some trees take hold where they do,
why others are singled out, snapped, charred.
A bud shoots open
before its time. This absence of your light
gives trees little to do.

∾

The keel steadies
under full cargo, full sails.
Three ducks arc over the mast.
You are gone.
I watch shipbuilders
lay down their tools.

THE KORL SCULPTOR

(after reading *Life in the Iron Mills,* by Rebecca Harding Davis)

Sleeping, he needs someone to break the fall
every time he turns over.
He takes a piece of tin.
Without waking, he sculpts the bend in his subject's fingers,
the glint in her eyes.
By day, he inscribes where sun
flares through the bars of his cell.
As the sun sets, etchings rise
in the hunched forms of furnace tenders—
reliefs from a time when he knew it best,

when furnaces stopped coughing up iron.
Tending done, the weight
of his shovel bore down on his chisel.
She walked far into every night,
lugging a pail of flitch
for his midnight supper.
Then she collapsed in the ash-heaps
where she became his bone-tired model.
There her dreams sifted and turned—
a red horse licked tufts of charcoal clouds.
They soared above
stack after stack of foundry flares.

As if a tailor drew thread,
she breathed,
he chipped
the flesh-tinted korl,

The figure, a coarse, sooty angel
held them up until one night
the directors toured the mill,
glared his work in to bold relief:

"See the instep's strained muscles,
its gnarled hands,
the questions of God it asks.
But what does it mean?"
The sculptor answered, "She be hungry."
For this, for showing what the chisel
can be to the dreamer,
he gouges her crouched figure onto walls,
tethered to a following sun.

ROTOGRAVURE

In the orchard, light from the west
hot-walks swallows
         who dodge and throng.
Their streaming wings slap at updrafts,
at apple boughs
         tangled with twilight.
As I lean on the gate,
         my husband and friend
dissolve down the path,
their footfall a precious balm.
Voices of skittish children
         hand spring across lawns,
glint like geodes rolling.

Leaning in to this
will not keep it, whatever arrests me
tumbles away in whispers.
Yet anything I press against—
         silty water brimming a moss-lined trough,
cocoons in newsprint tents,
         that soft pocking
of rain, my receding beloveds
turns me,
moves me, and I follow them.

GALAHAD BLUE

Strange, how the giving comes,
after I propped
the nearly snapped delphinium
with a whittled stick.
My husband vanishes
into the woods each day.
Light dapples him.
I lag behind, restless
for some blossom
to strut its color,
but most, now
hold out.

Except the delphinium.
Last spring when I planted it,
stunned such quiet rapture
opened in my yard.
It seemed pure nerve.
I wanted it everywhere.
Then air became dense,
as waiting finches
and sparrows flattened it.

Now only cardinals come,
at dawn and dusk.
I moved the delphinium
next to another—
its lavender flashes
flung open. As they faded,
I cut them back, and what remains

are seed-cases blackened
and wagging as cat-tails
imparting their breath.

I have been possessive,
of this transplanted Galahad blue,
with its buds bunched against
chill nights,
their hue of lowered sky.
While my husband, stilled by light
recedes farther up the path,
then returns, iron-warm,
and I pull him in, close.

BAY ROAD GARDEN

The thrush hums
a small canticle
while dusty-rose cosmos

lean on Jacob's ladder.
Hollyhocks list toward the wall.
Whoever dares tread this plot

where most grow knock-kneed
find leaf-edges
clamoring for light,

singed by early frost.
Over and over the eye
stirs a threnody in the heart.

Sometimes the delphinium
thwarts a second showing
from this season, or mallow

shirks the sun's work.
Then the brush of astilbe,
is gone by and bronzed.

I let them fall
in to neglect, cowed
by brighter, fuller gardens.

Blooms, dissolve into sepia,
contrast with deepening evergreens
as the solo note of lilies

blare out for only one day.
This play of shadow
and light is wily, moves

to the meadow
where waist-high goldenrod
verges on sweet timothy.

Here remains
the abandoned nest.
Here I long

to launch out, roam
in the scratched chord
of the thrush's desire call.

AVIAN RAPTURE

∾

Attraction brews
deep in the gut, spills
into opening wings,
and the syrinx runs
the entire body.

A trio of male doves
perch high,
outsing each other
all morning,
each one
reaches beyond clouds
for a tawny female.

The come-nest-with-me calls
become more resigned
as she retreats
to the underbrush.

She stays mute,
does not preen, for her drab
feathers attract as she roosts
on this limb of spring.

I did not see
the heart you drew
into snow, our initials
scribbling the drifts,
means I could not look out

on this harsh winter
that hurled a goshawk
into our yard.
We were stunned out of lunch
when we sighted him—
he blinded the snow.

We could not believe
he roosted so close.
Then I saw the limp form
he gorged on,
the blood-spackled snow,
swirls of feathers
still flicking.

Too late to save the dove,
you chased the hawk
out of view. He lifted up
with the dove dangling
from his obscene beak.

Later you covered
where his circling had stilled.

We blamed ourselves
for throwing millet into the open,
drawing dozens of doves.
Days after none came—
a cold snap kept them at bay.

Spring again,
a new nest has been built
And for this
I call out to you.

STRONGER THAN WINTER
(for Amy Clampitt)

I.

Early spring, that wait
for sleeve-rolling warmth.
I want to rush at my garden
like a horse careening newly greened fields,
then slow at the sight
of shoots poking holes through dead leaves.
This snow-washed air, the phoebe's call,
 warm enough for muddy knees.

I go there alone,
rake out dust and spent
stems from new shoots.
Each spring I must guess them—
ground-skulking clumps of venetian blinds
are Jacob's Ladder, scissor-kicking blades

are iris, flanked by stars
of bleeding hearts. Some hardier
than others; some I have forgotten.
When their tips jut up, I am knocked back,
not believing they survived, then worry over
what still hunkers below.
A long stretch from season to season,
memory whited out under record snows.

II.

I have yet to uncover the delphinium
from last season, the one
I transplanted for a better chance.
Nothing I uncover will replace it.
I clip, and dig, watchful,
for its star-shaped stalk.
No matter whites and lavenders
emerge, it's the Galahad blue I want,
the one the knighted my love.

A stubborn weed won't uproot.
I am wary spring is false.
My muttering rumbles.
Spinning from the day's revisions,
my husband is caught by the same urge
for sodden knees, the must of dirt.
But I want to settle my loss alone.

When he spots the foliage
of the delphinium I'd tended,
I let him rake around clumps
of evening primrose, not caring if they thin out.
Hoping he'll tire before he reaches
the nearly short-lived
Galahad blue I dare not touch,
I keep checking
as he closes in,
then leap to see how he leaves it—
upright, shaken out, gaining on the light.

III.

We put away our rakes, as your work
of blazing through form begins.
I imagine the danger—you
squinting hard at the shadowed edges
of new growth. Even darkness
can not scare off your appetite for naming.

The next morning I travel
from my side of this small range
to your reading. Your voice,
a scale of surprise.
Your poems praise
the consonantal loss of birdsong,
a merging of anniversaries. Your endings—
lingering bells.
When we first met, you called me
a fellow wanderer in Grasmere.

I've roamed there since in memory, turning
a gate into fields of foxgloves.
Today, you seem weary,
more delicate than usual. Still,
you are anxious
for what light has brought,
and when you step
over the border, you mine light,
quicken with its brightening.

IV.

You spring from bloodroot, leaves
wrapped cabbage-tight,
to the shuttered buds of trillium,
sing the rarity of red.
You say they are ready,
they have been waiting for this.

I think how deeply rooted
your trust is when you skitter off:
"Now it's a real garden!"
I join you by dutchmen's britches
you have not seen
since your childhood in Iowa.
As they lean into sun,
I think of my great-aunt's garden,
where I last saw them,

child-dazed by the tumble
of butternuts. She gave me
The Secret Garden, and in hers, I entered it,
dug for the rusted key that dissolved borders
of iris and columbine, until
we scoured the Green Mountains for lady-slippers,
lint spinning in fresh nests.

V.

She had your eye for the panicled flashing
in things. If she had written,
she would have led us down
paths of green. Somehow,
your poems let her continue.
And your Aunt Edith, showed you at four,
rose at the grosbeak's throat,
its medallion of passion.
Once in class, you passed a bird's nest
around a circle. Its hull

was lined with twigs and blonde hair.
After each of us held it, you dismissed us for the day.
Now each spring, I string low branches
with tufts of hair from my brush,
for birds. Under the relay of calls,
I let my husband rake.
I did not know he'd been waiting
for an embrace, I'd pushed him away.

I let in my husband's longing,
It will electrify the unbidden blooms.
Of late, a young male grosbeak is bold enough
to stay and feed. He coaxes out
his skittish mate who would not nest until now.

SO DOES THIS CANTICLE FOR WIND

Everywhere April skids, its release
$$\text{untimely and fickle.}$$
Spring peepers strum ponds
sudden with run-off, repeat
$$\text{cold, lonely births.}$$
The blackbird's tenuto unscrolls
in marshes, arches cattails back,
risks humility in spring.
The wrought-iron chair,
$$\text{supple from rust}$$
sinks into the rise.
I lean into this hush
$$\text{of breeze-tossed branches,}$$
and waiting becomes the psalm
of doing. Where there is thread,
there is tugging, a pulse
$$\text{slowed in your ways.}$$
I cuddle in the lull
like a handed-down shirt,
still sun-warmed from bending over my hoe.

Nearer the loosening to stoop so,
drop, at last, to dirt-scuffed knees.
These knees too soft, this garden
$$\text{too rocky}$$
defy the summons to bend.
Your return as uncertain as each day's seeming
$$\text{or a catch}$$
in the side— the spoon rest shattered again,

the mending futile, the spout
on the heirloom teapot cracked again,
so nothing for it but
                     to drop at last,
toughen my knees, cull stones from soil,
while above leaf-buds
keep their white-knuckled hold
                          on sky.

FOR A FEW TREES

Rather notice,
the trees
are wearing nametags.

They know the tourists are back
by the scent of city
fretting in their boughs.

Rather observe
their shoots lean steadily
toward the sun

like the old man
throwing
grain to pigeons.

Rather grasp
how they tilt
eavesdropping

on fishermen's words
cast off
stitch by stitch.

See how they stand!
So still, so full of trembling
as their apprenticeship resumes

by learning wind shifts
with gulls and kites
that careen each spring

above their tops!
See
how they swerve now

like tethered boats
in the current's
slight tug

then *relevé* headlong
in an updraft.
But observe

how they sometimes squat,
throw dice, shuffle cards.
Observe

one not included
off dancing.

QUICK TO BOLT

Last week evening primrose bloomed
under stutters of fireflies.
We needed no moon
as they stung blossoms
with blonde stripes of longing.
We dreamt of lilies
fishtailing stars,
lip-synched praises,
the readable heat lightening
of our amazement.

Then blossoms dropped the season.
Too much the vanishing held us
as we murmured, hovered, hoped for more.
Already late, we could not follow.
The vanishing flashed
quickly as a new bird underlit
with goldfinch tones,
the glint in your eye.

Call it lust, this need
for narrative in each new unfolding,
the musk of playing it out.
Unshaken as roots that send up
wave after wave of bloom,
we stood, waiting.
Then one late-firing primrose opened,
shivering, straggling, decanting sun.

꒱ III ꒰

PARTING SHOTS

Light quickens, trees lift,
            so I long
for warped glass to still
as I scan woods
            for that tawny light
in the underbrush
when deer rub the salt-lick.
Perhaps that's all we're given
            in the slow massing
of days when some residue of light
            gathers into the catch
and slip of movement and shades changing
are whole breaths
            that fog the glass
when first leaves blur, then form follows—
a pocked coat, a lapsing eye,
            the white heat
of the deers' tipped hind as they startle
into woods, shivers there
as trout might among spotted stones.

And so, within, hovers the unspeakable,
            where no rind or seed
will lure them to the moss-slick trough
where the silty water reflects a sun—
they are to themselves as we are.
But when each return marks
            the binocular case sprung
open on the coffee table,
I so need you

to include me
in their after-image, their mercy
since angels stopped huddling
                    around my bed
pushing one dream into the next.
If the deer come
trembling with distance,
will we close in on our straying,
and if that be given,
how, how then, can we let them
                    steal away?

UNCERTAIN PERCHES

I fed the mare grass
from the other side of the fence.
She was testy, fly-swarmed,
shunned her filly
who was rooting at her teats
in record June heat.
I pulled up lanky, lush stalks,
sweetened the mix
with just-opened clover.

I held the ground-dampened tips
to her mouth, stroked
her soft underlip.
Solace in the velvet-held whiskers there.
Glimpses of many childhood horses,
the sibilance of their nicknames.
The lure of bays and chestnuts
unshaken through early middle age.
Cradling their muzzles
was enough and again enough.

When the mare slobbered the stalks,
chewed them with what
must have sounded like the roar
of twin engines to our daughter,
and she reached for that nose
slathered with green foam,
giggled as that great jaw
circled, I thought my past life
with its former loves

was leading to this moment
when she could touch the other.

Or so I needed to imagine it was—
each step stretching
to plentitude, each love
converting its purpose.
In truth, she would not touch,
not yet, rather, wanted
to see me hold
the savor of each blade under the mare's nose.
The filly latched on and nursed,
the mare content now to let down, suckling
deafening as cicadas rising in mid-day sun.

I became all mammal then: that
heeding and needing to be elsewhere
while our young find succor
in pulling us close.
And in truth,
when my daughter weans herself
to greet the great "what's next,"
I will miss the sweep
of her hand across my breast,
the sough of milk-soothed sleep.

MILO

She made me drive by
one more time,

hoping we'd sight him
grazing, grass not yet

frost-razed that balmy
late December afternoon.

Sweatshirt weather.
We saw him walking

towards his new barn
ears forward, marching

the ride's end.
I saw each footfall

each measured flexion,
felt the swing

of his back, his owner
there instead of me.

Loose reins. That kind
Of closure. She said

he looked content.
I said they wouldn't

move him to a place where
where it would be otherwise.

That night I couldn't fill
the loss of him

with anything I knew.
He'd held every little grief

at bay while
I'd ridden him,

the worry, the too-many times
her father showed up drunk

mid-afternoon to watch me
ride. He could never

follow me
to the far field

where I galloped.
Once I draped

over Milo's neck,
crushed every hollow

of his ears, and he
strode on,

his oat-breath a balm
in that golden-meadowed hour.

INSOMNIA

Lights show
   under scrolled dormers
of the old folks' home
   as I make a second pass
for milk in the chill heart
   of a sleepless night.
I am edgy from the high wire
   of playoffs: the relief gave up the lead
the starter was two outs from . . .
   I have counted a baker's dozen
awake across the way.
   They are not fitful,
but I cannot fall into
   a soothing pool of sleep.

One man skunked on solitaire
   looks back fast for referees,
then trips the right jack face-up,
   breaks the impasse,
slaps the deck
   into four slick piles.
That jack smirks from the deck
   as the man reshuffles,
keen on beating his record.

   Another man in an overstuffed chair,
two covered parrot cages
   at his side, all before the T.V.
Its blue glare fires
   replays of home runs

that strobe the room.
 Nothing budges
as light's quick friction
 of the tying run
shoots through him.

 As I scan other lit windows:
one bends over botanical plates
 traces the outline of each jagged stem,
another blots light, rocks her cat.
 I wonder if anyone came to claim
the woman who died next to me
 in that hospital room,
who all night
 kept asking if the Red Sox won,
if it was morning yet,
 who found the right
to die by dawn.
 I wonder if she bridged
that stillness without dread.

FOR THE FEAST OF THE EPIPHANY

Mourning doves are mired in snowy boughs.
Knots of spare song
within their buffed chests
steady them against cold.
They lean toward each other,
heads cloaked by wings.

Yesterday, my husband hauled
the Christmas tree deep into the woods.
As the stripped limbs eclipsed his form,
my heart dragged on the ground
with the point of the fallen tree.

We postpone ousting it from our house,
until its boughs yellow
and the gift-bearing travelers kneel.
This year was a hard search,
long into darkness, during first snow.
At last, a Douglas fir
in the west window shed its embered scent.

This year my gift ornament
was a pewter dove, wings hurled
open, as if troubling a descent
to peace. It glinted off red-ribboned trumpets,
caroling cherubs, wayward birds.
Outside, doves are lifting off.
Snow shimmies, lost to itself for good.

MORNING ENOUGH

When fog hugs
an inland river
its every curve,

then lifts off, unscrolls
over fields, (the river's
imprint still intact),

I think I've seen enough
until I make
the entrance ramp:

the gaining sun
hangs off a far jag
of the eastward-leaning range

like slub gold;
fog decants light,
casts the sky shell-pink.

This morning the commute
all but drives itself,
crossing this river

until traffic clogs.
I wait,
think back to other mornings

stopped by a risen drawbridge
on a tidal-fed river.
Leaning over the bridge gates

I watched tugs
heave against an oil tanker,
turn its bow seaward.

That grating ballet
never scraped shore,
though it took the width of the river

to get that much right.
As they passed,
diesel smudged the air,

pressed against the fog,
which blew in wisps
off tidal feed.

Still I waited there
for the river to settle
into its most visible quiet,

until fog thickened for a moment,
then rose, stenciled
the bridge's grid.

Remembering such lifting
I roll local names
for haze over my tongue—

"riverfog," "seasmoke,",
give thanks for the wild
skirmishes of words,

their little inlets
drifting this far.

FRESHENING

Pendulous cows
nose for the right dosage
of sky in hay racks.
My brother works

the line, skitters
from trough to stanchion
between each pair
of lean-to hips.

Visor of his John Deere hat
turned so he can lay
his ear flush
with each one's side.

He hears the soft thunder
in each mellow belly
as the blessed
white stream releases.

And all is dunked
in the odor
of a dairy's brewery—
ferment of clover and bloat,

vescue and timothy,
mouldering silage,
the readiness
to freshen.

I walk up and down the aisle
carrying my newborn niece.
I am more tentative
holding her wobbly body

than I was bottle-feeding
an hour-old
birth-slick heifer
moments before.

I think of the odd grace
siphoned from
these broody cows—
that we are the first

to taste their beesting,
not their rooting,
eager, young.
As I rock my niece,

this entire low-ceilinged barn
ticks to the milk machine's
rhythm, this biding with design.

FARMER BY THE SEA

No one will go in.
The couple testing it
wade just above
the breath-shucking chill
that eases the body in.

The woman verges more,
arms open, sharpening
the point of her dive,
daring the man
or the gathering tide
to dunk her at last.

Perhaps the farmer imagines her
resurfacing spaniel-slick and birth-wet,
suit clinging,
breasts highlighted
by the sea's dense caress.

The angle of his gaze,
lax curve
in the small of his back,
the way his calves thrill to the sand's grit
lead me to believe this.

He looks out and out, pleased
with his easeful contours on the beach,
while his wife and daughter
dig for clams; his wife
who has not hiked up her skirt in years,
now ankle-deep and dreaming.

ANY WONDER

For weeks now, the talk
has been of trees.
Their slow fade is unruly—
in one stand anywhere,

maples' charging colors
still bay at the horizon,
and may brighten yet—
the sudden brilliance of fire-knots.

Then the poplar already blasted
of cover, pokes low-slung clouds,
and the oak, a bleared gutter hue
that comes after days of rain.

The sycamore holds out,
untested by change in light.
As it delivers its green,
conifers keep flaunting their ever-ness.

Far be it from any of us—
we're working on theories—
the secretary who's aged
so quickly of late is stopped

by variations in a single tree—
why some leaves are swept by a firebrand
first, why others leer at light.
She's written her daughters.

They send bouquets, but no answers,
and so she rummages,
traces the weight each branch must bear,
how long it served as a perch,

how many crickets thrummed its base.
We take her with us
as we take in whole avenues
late afternoon. Light diminishes the hills,

and we agree this autumn has lolled on,
orchard-heavy. These sap-golden days
are disquieting; this breach of green
and yellow has side-stepped
the ghostly paring away.
We miss the sharp air turning sharper,
frost's plumage on panes,
the rush in foliage, its stained adamance.

FEEDING STATIONS

Rainy morning, goldfinches jump-started the gray.
Those tiny bodies glowed
like divots of electricity,
when a male finch smacked
into the picture window, hit hard
by the would-be forest behind.

On the commute, I thought of all the dull-colored females,
who hit, came out of that blow
minutes later, thought how the showy males
get taken sooner, perhaps the price
of carrying sun
too close to the heart.

I called home and heard,
"At 8:38 this morning, the goldfinch flew away!"
began class, when one student remarked,
"You seem up. Did you win the lottery?"
"Oh no. Something better,"
told them of the morning,

how this year more goldfinches
have come and stayed on,
their breeze-struck muttering
always a backdrop,
their phosphorescent bodies
glint like marquee from another life.

Had the goldfinch not lived,
there would not have been

a story, it came alive
in the telling, my students' slowed breathing
catching it, though they must think me
some eccentric bird lady—hunkering

in nightie and wellies, muddy-kneed
with binoculars, stealing up
on the great what-is.
Somehow they like my garden stories—
the competition for seed and nest,
a way to go on, as narrative

is the human way to go on,
and I told it again,
this time with my students included
to an elderly friend who waits
in the too-clean nursing home,
listens to snips from visitors' lives,

and when I finished
she said, "Now that is a good story."
And told it again to a friend who waits
for a garden with trellises that tilt heavenward.
He told me of holding a crashed
hummingbird once, thought it

dead until its tongue
probed for honey held
in his palm, fed on
that strangeness, then zigged off.
This evening the grosbeak
who has taken four seasons

to bring his mate, looks everywhere
as he trills, squabbles, while she listens
pleased with their need to remain.
The towhee stops whistling once
he's perched on a limb,
no longer ground-spavined.

His register traces the going
and the coming back
rhapsodic and full—
Two names thinned
from the traffic of birdsong,
resplendent in the half-light of dawn and dusk.

THE ANGEL'S DOSSIER

∾

In a museum open late, case after case
of butterfly wings, miraculous contrast:

royal blue satin edged with goldenrod spots,
black veins shot through with vermilion.

This bursting from a still world, dark within
a tissue chrysalis to one of spinning brilliance.

There is one visitor who lags,
tries to touch color just inches below him.

("How can satin be so thin? Someone dusted
in reverse, dusted sheen *onto* wings.")

Those wings shudder after he has passed,
but catch in the outskirts of vision,

make him wonder if what he saw
was a play of light. He turns back,

finds them quaking.
Unlike a watch which is opened

because wings can't shiver on their own.

The watchmaker bends over his bench,
works in an amber light.

Gear-flint sloughs off like shavings
at a whittler's feet.

Springs, bolts, faces without hands
like beach salvage, the wings

impossible to pin without quaking.
So the residue accumulates,

sets out for a deepening
mystery, or a sign—

"No mystery here."
He pieces the watch back,

then taps for a true tick—a balance
between gust and lull.

There are moons during day—new pears
stud branches in late summer.

The same women gather underneath,
fill their aprons with the hard, sour, fruit,

dust the day clear with a goosewing,
begin to soften the skin.

Pears too hard for jam or butter,
but in time yield to the sweet ferment of brandy.

Soon the women will raid the pulp,
line their shelves with dated jars,

rotate them according to light,
wonder when they can press an essence through.

They soften the skin by gossiping
about the hurricane that just missed town.

Talk is of waiting—whether the eye
is most furious, how the windows were braced

with tape cross stitches. When the fringe blew in,
none of them saw the pear tree

was scattered enough to hold fast,
its moons as reliable as the watchmaker's lens.

The way a drop of rain clings
to fruit after clouds move off,

captures the first peering of sun,
reflects the world in a clear bead.

What presents itself can not
stay or leave, absolutely, unless shaken.

The way wind lifts above, dunks
under thin sheets, cradles a sleeper,

shags light through spruces—
spinning off, fusing, showing

five tones of green, the mournful creak
of doves' wings brace against it overhead.

All this fills the room until wind steals away
and the real pounces on the sleeper who turns,

just coming awake, watches calm
bat the shade pull at the window.

When sun hits, strews
reflected light all over the room,

the sleeper is caught in the grace
of not knowing how that drop survived overnight.

SCENT OF ROSES, SALT AIR

Rosa rugosa, just shingles of pink,
quartets of petals

                spell *possible*,

as my daughter spills
on to the beach packed

            with sea-dredge

she must have: crab pinchers, fish spine or head,
twine, bottle caps, rocks buffed
to purple or pink, shells glistened

              by waves.

By day's end her pail
tips, brimful.
She asks for my hand to hold

          her trove.

I give it
though I doubt my hand
is steady enough.
I am taken

        from her play,

can't shake my stunted garden back home.
Where is my tumble

        of blossom,

my throng of color?
My hands, cracked from dirt
as I kneaded caches of minerals
into sand, sifted out stones,
tamped out a cove for each slip.
I delved with same abandon she shucked
salvage from sand.

I earned their keep.
Yet only pinches of color

        sprang up.

Back on the porch splintered by wind,
she dumps her shards,
names each again as favorite.
A glimpse south holds the Sankaty Head Lighthouse,
A sweep of light—
and with it hints of clearing.

        She sees dogs chasing
and mare's tails in clouds.
I want this to be with me,
want to know

      what I tend will grow.
No doubt happiness can hold here, sure
as clouds and finicky winds

        can whisk away sorrow.

Later, in town, the ferry rumbles.
My daughter stops by an easel set

      before the harbor.
An artist's hand is raised.
One stroke there could soften
a rising tide.
Another stroke here tumbles roses

        to the foreground
that untrainable pink of roses,
loosed from the trellis,
spilling off the branch.

ABOUT THE AUTHOR

MARY FISTER teaches writing and literature at the University of Hartford, and has for over thirty years. Her family has roots in Vermont that go all the way back to the DAR, but she was born in the Midwest when her Dad started his first job, and so she will forever be a "flatlander." She earned an MFA from the University of Massachusetts. Her poems have appeared in journals such as *Ploughshares, The Massachusetts Review, Tar River Poetry,* and *Volt* among many others. Her chapbook, *Provenance of the Lost* was published by Finishing Line Press. She lives in Northampton, Massachusetts, with her beloved kitties BooDah, Maibee, a bunny, Ella, and a horse, Milli.